THE ULTIMATE ANIMAL LIBRARY

Armadillos

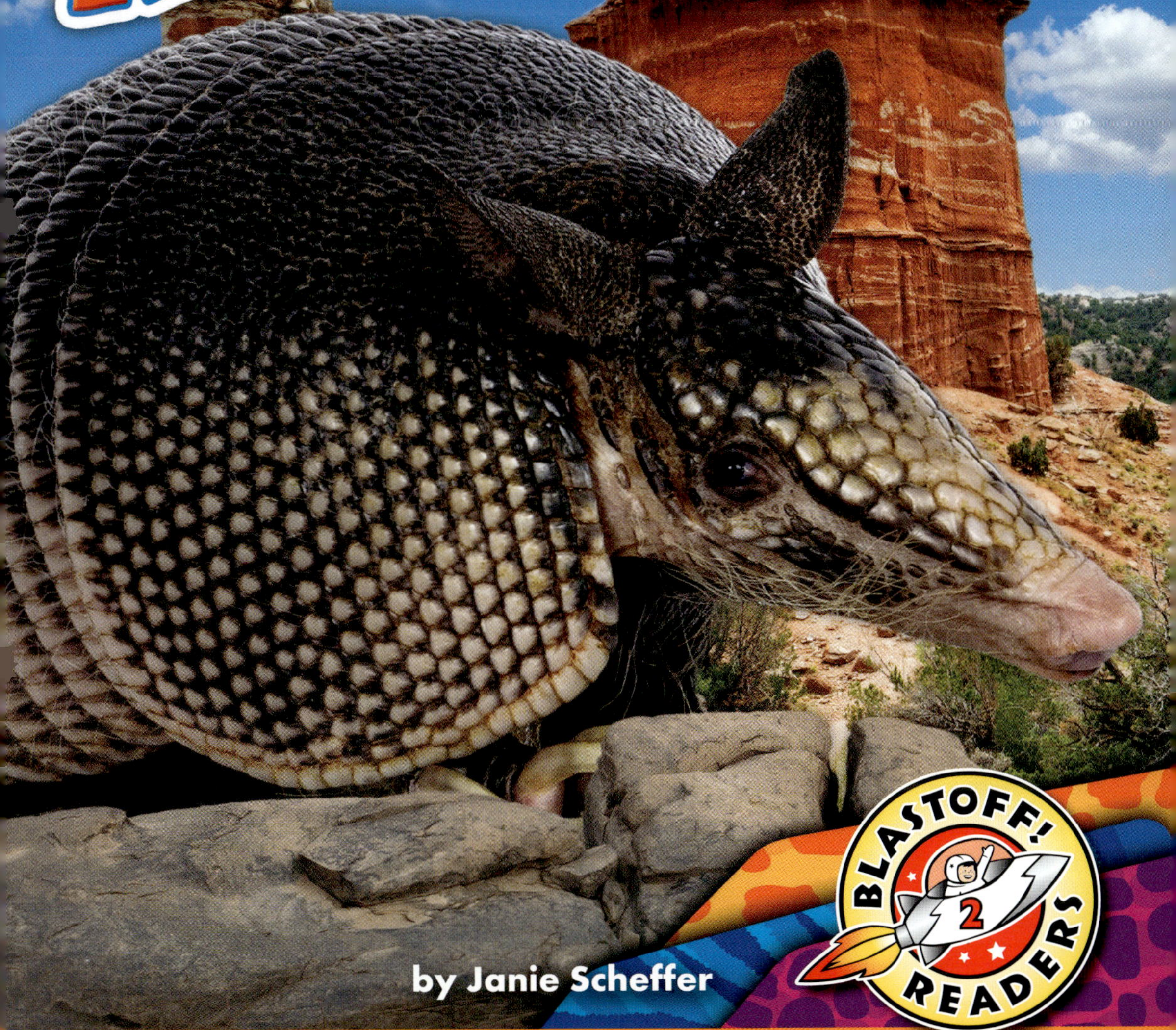

by Janie Scheffer

BLASTOFF! READERS 2

BLASTOFF! READERS, AN IMPRINT OF BELLWETHER MEDIA BY FLUTTERBEE

Blastoff! Readers are carefully developed by literacy experts to build reading stamina and move students toward fluency by combining standards-based content with developmentally appropriate text.

LEVELS

Level 1 provides the most support through repetition of high-frequency words, light text, predictable sentence patterns, and strong visual support.

Level 2 offers early readers a bit more challenge through varied sentences, increased text load, and text-supportive special features.

Level 3 advances early-fluent readers toward fluency through increased text load, less reliance on photos, advancing concepts, longer sentences, and more complex special features.

★ **Blastoff! Universe**

Reading Level

Blastoff! Beginners — Grade K

Blastoff! Readers — Grades 1–3

Blastoff! Discovery — Grade 4

This edition first published in 2027 by Bellwether Media, Inc.

For information regarding permission, write to Bellwether Media, Inc., Attention: Permissions Department, 3500 American Blvd W, Suite 150, Bloomington, MN 55431.

Library of Congress Cataloging-in-Publication Data

Names: Scheffer, Janie, 1992- author
Title: Armadillos / by Janie Scheffer.
Description: Minneapolis, Minnesota : Bellwether Media, Inc., 2027. | Series: Ultimate animal library | Includes bibliographical references and index. | Audience: Ages 5-8 | Audience: Grades 2-3 | Summary: "Relevant images match informative text in this introduction to armadillos. Intended for students in kindergarten through third grade"-- Provided by publisher.
Identifiers: LCCN 2026013890 (print) | LCCN 2026013891 (ebook) | ISBN 9798898800390 (library binding) | ISBN 9798898801632 (ebook)
Subjects: LCSH: Armadillos
Classification: LCC QL737.E23 S37 2027 (print) | LCC QL737.E23 (ebook)
LC record available at https://lccn.loc.gov/2026013890
LC ebook record available at https://lccn.loc.gov/2026013891

Editor: Elizabeth Neuenfeldt   Designer: Brittany McIntosh

Printed in the United States of America, North Mankato, MN.

Table of Contents

What Are Armadillos?

Armadillos are **mammals**. There are around 20 different armadillo **species**. They live in North, Central, and South America.

Nine-banded Armadillo Report

Range

Status in the Wild

Habitats

Armadillos are different sizes. Giant armadillos weigh up to 71 pounds (32 kilograms).

giant armadillo

Pink fairy armadillos weigh up to 0.5 pounds (0.2 kilograms).

Armadillos have rounded shells.
Their shells have hard bands
made of bone.

Armadillos are different colors.
They can be yellow, brown,
pink, gray, or black.

Armadillos have fur or hair on their sides and bellies. Some have hair on their backs too.

Armadillos have strong, short legs. They have long, sharp claws.

How to Spot an Armadillo

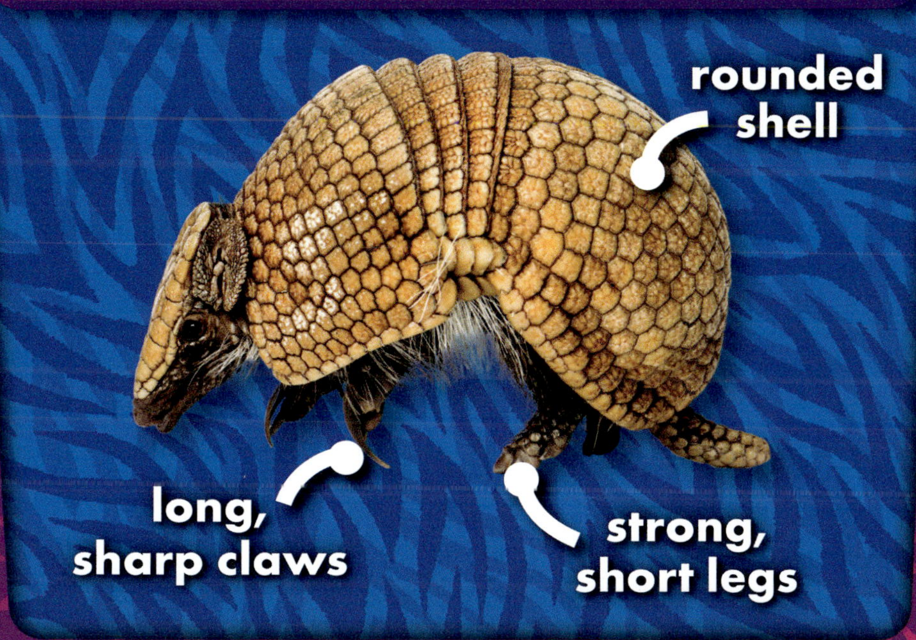

Smell and Dig!

Armadillos mostly live in warm **wetlands**. Some live in forests or **shrublands**.

Most make **burrows** in logs and grass. Some make burrows underground.

In warmer months, armadillos mostly live alone. They hunt at night.

When it is cold, they sometimes group together. They may hunt during the day.

Armadillos are **insectivores**. They smell for **prey**. Then they dig for it.

Armadillos hide from **predators** in their burrows or their shells.

Growing Up

Female armadillos give birth to up to 12 **pups** at a time.

Pups are born with soft shells. They feel like leather.

Most pups can roll into balls hours after birth. Days later, their shells harden.

Pups stay with mom for up to one year. They can live for up to 30 years!

Life of an Armadillo

Name of Babies

pups

Number of Babies

up to 12

Time Spent with Mom

up to 1 year

Life Span

up to 30 years

Glossary

burrows—tunnels or holes in the ground used as animals' homes

insectivores—animals that only eat insects; insects are small animals with six legs and bodies divided into three parts.

mammals—warm-blooded animals that have backbones and feed their young milk

predators—animals that hunt other animals for food

prey—animals that are hunted by other animals for food

pups—baby armadillos

shrublands—dry grasslands that have mostly low plants and few trees

species—kinds of an animal

wetlands—areas of land that are covered with low levels of water for most of the year

To Learn More

AT THE LIBRARY

Rex, Ruby. *Inside an Armadillo's Burrow.* Minneapolis, Minn.: Bearport Publishing Company, 2023.

Schuh, Mari. *Baby Turtle or Baby Armadillo?* Minneapolis, Minn.: Bellwether Media, 2026.

Watt, Melanie E. *Nine-banded Armadillo.* New York, N.Y.: Lightbox Learning, 2025.

ON THE WEB

FACTSURFER

Factsurfer.com gives you a safe, fun way to find more information.

1. Go to www.factsurfer.com.
2. Enter "armadillos" into the search box and click 🔍.
3. Select your book cover to see a list of related content.

Index

The images in this book are reproduced through the courtesy of: Nynke van Holten, front cover (armadillo), p. 23; Zack Frank, front cover (background), pp. 2-3; Eric Isselee, pp. 3, 11; melissamn, p. 4; Kevin Schafer/ Getty Images, p. 6; Harsha_Madusanka, p. 7; slowmotiongli, p. 8; CapturingLight.Photo, p. 9; Joel Trick, p. 10; RollingEarth, pp. 10-11; guentermanaus, p. 12; Wirestock Creators, p. 13; Karel Bartik, p. 14; Reto Buehler, p. 15; DUOTONE, pp. 16-17; Sergey Demo SVDPhoto, p. 17 (coyote); Holly Kuchera, p. 17 (bobcat); Jim Schwabel, p. 17 (alligator); Alizada Studios, p. 17 (armadillo); Bradley Rentz/ Wikimedia Commons, p. 17 (ant); Patrick Coin/ Wikimedia Commons, p. 17 (beetle); DJack, p. 17 (cricket); Manoel, p. 18; belizar, pp. 18-19, 20; Rosanne Tackaberry/ Alamy Stock Photo, p. 21.